Robert Milligan is ranked as a leading silk in both Legal 500 and Chambers UK and is rated as the Star Individual for Personal Injury work in Chambers UK. He has a particular interest in product liability claims, fatal claims and catastrophic injuries. He was instructed by the defenders in the Vioxx litigation and acts for the pursuers in the group litigations relating to metal on metal hips, diesel emissions and vaginal mesh implants. He speaks and writes regularly on personal injury related matters, particularly in relation to damages.

Robert is a legal chairman of the War Pensions Appeal Tribunal and sits on the SRU Discipline Panel. In 2017 he represented the Scotland player Ryan Wilson following an incident in the Calcutta Cup match of that year. He is a member of the Scottish Civil Justice Council Working Group on Group Proceedings.

Funding Personal Injury Litigation in Scotland

Funding Personal Injury Litigation in Scotland

Robert Milligan QC
Compass Chambers, Faculty of Advocates
Dip LP (Edinburgh); MCI Arb

Law Brief Publishing

Published 2021 by Law Brief Publishing, an imprint of Law Brief Publishing Ltd
30 The Parks
Minehead
Somerset
TA24 8BT

www.lawbriefpublishing.com

Paperback: 978-1-912687-79-4

CONTENTS

CHAPTER ONE

INTRODUCTION

When I started my traineeship with a well-known litigation firm in Edinburgh in 1992 most cases in the Court of Session were personal injuries actions funded either by legal aid or trade unions, with a few legally-aided cases thrown in for good measure. Otherwise, the prohibitive expenses (costs) of court actions put litigation beyond the reach of all but the wealthiest of individuals.

As pressure grew on the Scottish Legal Aid Board's budget and union membership declined, interest grew in other means of funding court cases as a means of improving access to justice for individual members of the public. In particular, legal expenses insurance became more common. This was initially mostly "before the event" insurance, usually from motor insurance or home insurance polices. In due course, this was largely supplanted by "after the event" ("ATE") insurance, whereby the pursuer pays a premium, usually from the proceeds of a successful claim.

The main problem with this was the long-standing prohibition on lawyers taking fees calculated by reference to the damages awarded. To get round this, far-sighted legal firms set up claims management firms to provide the funding. The boards of these companies comprised the partners of the firms involved. In this way, lawyers could receive a percentage cut of the damages, so long as they did so in their capacity as a claims manager rather than legal advisor.

The Civil Litigation (Expenses and Group Proceedings) (Scotland) Act 2018 ("the 2018 Act") is the logical conclusion of this process, enabling solicitors to provide a "no win, no fee" service to clients in return for enhanced payments in the event of a successful outcome.

More radically still, the 2018 Act has introduced a system of qualified one-way costs shifting ("QOCS") that protects pursuers from adverse findings of expenses in the event that they are unsuccessful.

The 2018 Act has been a long time in coming and wasn't fully implemented until mid 2021 but the ramifications will be felt for a long time to come. This work attempts to anticipate some of the major questions that will arise in practice, by reference to existing caselaw and developments in other jurisdictions. Particular attention is paid to the risks that still exist in funding personal injuries litigation, as the reforms should certainly not be seen as a blank cheque for pursuers.

The law stated here is as at 1st August 2021.

CHAPTER TWO

HISTORICAL BACKGROUND

Scots law has never prevented lawyers from acting on a "no win, no fee" basis. However, any bonus for acting in this way had to be limited to an uplift in fees charged, subject to a maximum of 100% (section 61A of the Solicitors (Scotland) Act 1980 and section 36 of the Law Reform (Miscellaneous Provisions) (Scotland) Act 1990).

An agreement to act in return for a percentage of the damages was not actually prohibited, but it was unenforceable on the basis that it was a *pactum de quota litis*. See *Quantum Claims Compensation Specialists Ltd v Powell* 1998 SC 316, where it was held that that the rule that a *pactum de quota litis* was unenforceable was limited in its application to solicitors who have undertaken professional obligations, so that a solicitor acting in a different capacity would be able to enforce the agreement.

Furthermore, premiums for ATE insurance have never been recoverable in Scotland (see *McNairs Exrx v Wrights Insultation Co Ltd* 2003 SLT 1311 and *McGraddie v McGraddie* (No.2) 2015 SC (UKSC) 45). Accordingly, it was difficult for the pursuer to find an affordable means of protection against any adverse finding in expenses.

The Report of the Scottish Civil Courts Review 2009 ("the Gill Report") contained a whole chapter in Volume 2 on the question of cost and funding of litigation. The original intention was that reform of the expenses regime in Scotland would go hand in hand with court reform. In the event, the Review of Expenses and Funding of Civil Litigation in Scotland 2013 ("the Taylor Report") took much longer to implement than the reform of the civil courts. Indeed, the most important reforms in relation costs and funding have taken over 10 years to come into place.

The first piece of major legislation was the 2018 Act, which paved the way for damages-based agreements and qualified one way cost shifting ("QOCS"). Even then, the regulations implanting those changes did not come into force until April 2020 and June 2021 respectively.

CHAPTER THREE

CIVIL LEGAL AID

3.1 <u>Introduction</u>

A comprehensive analysis of civil legal aid is well beyond the scope of this book, but there are a number of key points that should be recognised.

The first is that legal aid remains an important option for many forms of civil litigation, including family actions and certain clinical negligence actions, particularly those involving injuries caused during birth. The position in this respect is very different from England and Wales.

The second is that legal aid rates remain far below commercial market rates. Legal aid is attractive for lawyers taking on difficult cases with a significant risk that the claim will fail but far less attractive in cases that are likely to succeed. On the other hand, from a pursuer's perspective, the attraction lies in the form of funding that does not involve the loss of any damages (although the Scottish Legal Aid Board may require a financial contribution, depending on the pursuer's resources). This can create a serious conflict of interest for the lawyer.

The third is that where a lawyer takes on a case using legal aid, there may still be the option of recovering expenses from the other side instead of making a claim on the fund. This can often overcome the second point noted above. If legal aid is a safety net in the event of failure, there is still the possibility of recovery at commercial market rates, at least in relation to judicially recoverable fees.

The fourth is that legal aid takes a number of forms. Advice and Assistance covers office-based work and does not extend to court work. It is defined in section 6 of the Legal Aid (Scotland) Act 1986 ("the 1986 Act") as follows:

> ""Advice and assistance" means any of the following
>
> (a) oral or written advice provided to a person by a solicitor (or, where appropriate, by counsel)
>
> > (i) on the application of Scots law to any particular circumstances which have arisen in relation to the person seeking the advice;
> >
> > (ii) as to any steps which that person might appropriately take (whether by way of settling any claim, instituting, conducting or defending proceedings, making an agreement or other transaction, making a will or other instrument, obtaining further legal or other advice and assistance, or otherwise) having regard to the application of Scots law to those circumstances;
>
> (b) assistance provided to a person by a solicitor (or, where appropriate, by counsel) in taking any steps mentioned in paragraph (a)(ii) above, by taking such steps on his behalf or by assisting him in so taking them."

Court proceedings are covered by Civil Legal Aid. There is also Assistance by Way of Representation although that is not relevant here.

The distinction between the various forms of civil legal aid has been criticised by the Law Society of Scotland which has argued for a simplified scheme involving a single continuing grant (see *Legal Assistance in Scotland Fit for The 21st Century* Law Society of Scotland

Recommendations May 2015). However, *Rethinking Legal Aid An Independent Strategic Review* by Martyn Evan in February 2018 was generally positive about the current position and there is little prospect of imminent reform. It is interesting to note that spending on legal aid has fallen from a peak of £161M in 2010/11 to £136M in 2016/17 and is anticipated to continue falling. Of that £136M, only £40.9M was spent on civil legal assistance which would again suggest that this is not a priority for the Scottish Government.

3.2 Financial eligibility

In terms of section 15 of the 1986 Act there is an assessment of both capital and income, with the assets of a co-habiting partner also taken into account. For Advice and Assistance the capital threshold is £1,716. For Civil Legal Aid, the maximum capital to qualify for an award is £13,017. If the applicant and their partner has less than that in capital, there is a test of disposable income. The threshold for Advice and Assistance is disposable income of £12,740 and for Civil Legal Aid it is £26,239.

Where the applicant has a disposable income of more than £3,521, there is a sliding scale of contributions. Between £3,522 and £11,540, the contribution is 33%. Between £11,541 and £15,743 the contribution is 50%. Between £15,744 and £26,239 the contribution is 100%. The main benefit to the applicant when the contribution is 100% is that the solicitor will only be able to charge legal aid rates as opposed to normal commercial rates. In all cases

3.3 Probable cause

Section 14 of the 1986 Act provides as follows:

> "**14.** (1) Subject to section 15 of this Act and to subsections (1F) and (2) below, civil legal aid shall be available to a person if, on an application made to the Board
>
> (a) the Board is satisfied that he has a probabilis causa litigandi; and
>
> (b) it appears to the Board that it is reasonable in the particular circumstances of the case that he should receive legal aid.

This means that assuming the pursuer is financially eligible for legal aid, they still need to show *probabilis causa litigandi* or probable cause. This is not the same thing as a likelihood of success on a percentage basis. *Probabilis causa* is defined in the Taylor Report as "sufficient grounds for commencing legal action".

In its advice to legal aid applicants updated June 2018 the Scottish Legal Aid Board gave the following examples of when it would not be reasonable in the particular circumstances of a case to grant legal aid: "*it may not be reasonable to grant legal aid if the person you are trying to sue has no money, your case will cost much more than it is worth, it looks unlikely that you will succeed, you are using the wrong court, or if you have not fully considered other ways of sorting out the problem, before you take court action.*"

CHAPTER FOUR

SPECULATIVE ACTIONS AND CONTINGENCY FEES

4.1 <u>The old rules</u>

This method of funding has really come to the fore since the turn of the century. The vast majority of personal injury litigation in Scotland is now funded by the lawyers acting on a no win, no fee basis. Initially the idea was that the lawyers would charge a success fee, in the form of increased fees, to make up for the cases that are unsuccessful. However, as competition increased, it became increasingly uncommon for lawyers to charge an uplift in trade union work, on the basis that the vast majority of claims are resolved with a finding of expenses in favour of the pursuer. Indeed, many trade unions made it a condition that lawyers taking on their work would not charge their members any uplift to ensure 100% recovery. Some went even further and only engaged firms who were prepared to do other legal work, such as employment disputes, for free, in return for instructions in personal injury work.

In more contentious forms of work, law firms set up claims companies to underwrite litigation, in return for a damages-based agreement, as noted above.

This model has proved successful in increasing access to justice for pursuers who would not qualify for legal aid and do not have trade union backing. However, it has been entirely unregulated which means that pursuers sometimes sign away a significant proportion of their damages, even in a case where there is very little risk for the funder. As a result, it was a key recommendation of the Taylor

Review that lawyers should be allowed to enter into such agreements directly with the client.

4.2 Success fee agreements / damages based agreements

This position was simplified by Section 1 of the 2018 Act which provides as follows:

> **"1 Success fee agreements**
>
> (1) In this Part, a *"success fee agreement"* is an agreement between a person providing relevant services (the "provider") and the recipient of those services (the "recipient") under which the recipient—
>
>> (a) is to make a payment (the "success fee") to the provider in respect of the services if the recipient obtains a financial benefit in connection with a matter in relation to which the services are provided, but
>>
>> (b) is not to make any payment, or is to make a payment of a lower amount than the success fee, in respect of the services if no such benefit is obtained.
>
> (2) In this section—
>
> *"claims management services"* means services consisting of the provision of advice or services, other than legal services, in connection with the making of a claim for damages or other financial benefit, including—
>
>> (a) advice or services in relation to—
>>
>>> (i) legal representation,

(ii) the payment or funding of costs associated with making the claim,

(b) referring or introducing one person to another,

(c) making inquiries,

"legal services" means services consisting of the provision of legal advice, assistance or representation,

"payment" includes a transfer of assets and any other transfer of money's worth,

"relevant services" means legal services or claims management services provided in connection with a matter—

(a) which is the subject of civil proceedings to which the recipient is a party before a Scottish court or tribunal, or

(b) in relation to which such proceedings are in contemplation,

"Scottish court or tribunal" means a court or tribunal established under the law of Scotland.

(3) In this Part, the following terms, in relation to a success fee agreement, are to be construed in accordance with this section—

"payment",

"provider",

"recipient",

"relevant services",

"success fee".

In other words, lawyers can now enter enforceable damages-based agreements directly with their clients without the need to set up a separate claims company.

The Civil Litigation (Expenses and Group Proceedings) (Scotland) Act 2018 (Success Fee) Regulations 2020 ("the 2020 Regulations") came into force on 27th April 2020 (see The Civil Litigation (Expenses and Group Proceedings) (Scotland) Act 2018 (Commencement No 2 and Transitional Provision) Regulations 2020) and provided various limits on what the success fee agreement can cover:

4.3 Limits on the success fee

Regulation 2 of the 2020 Regulations provides as follows:

"**2.— Success fee cap**

(1) Subject to section 4 (power to cap success fees) of the 2018 Act, a success fee agreement must not require the recipient of relevant services to pay to the provider a success fee which, including VAT, exceeds the maximum amount provided for by these Regulations ("the success fee cap").

(2) The success fee cap is determined by reference to the financial benefit obtained by the recipient ("the financial benefit").

(3) In a matter that is, or could become, a claim for damages for personal injuries or the death of a person from personal injuries, the success fee cap is—

(a) in respect of the first £100,000 of the financial benefit, 20%,

(b) in respect of the amount of the financial benefit over £100,000 but not exceeding £500,000, 10%,

(c) in respect of the amount of the financial benefit over £500,000, 2.5%.

(4) In a matter that is, or could become, the subject of proceedings before an employment tribunal, the success fee cap is 35% of the financial benefit.

(5) In any other matter to which these Regulations apply, the success fee cap is 50% of the financial benefit.

(6) Where in connection with the same matter a recipient receives relevant services from more than one provider, whether under one or more success fee agreements, the success fee cap applies to the total amount payable by the recipient to those providers.

This important regulation provides for a series of caps on the amount of the success fee recoverable in a personal injury action. For the first £100,000 of "financial benefit" the limit is 20%; between £100,000 and £500,000 it is 10% and thereafter 2.5%. Accordingly, for an award of £750,000 the success fee could not exceed £20,000 + £40,000 + £6,250 = £66,250.

It is important to note that the regulations talk about the "financial benefit" rather than award of damages, which would suggest that if an award of £750,000 was made subject to a deduction of 50% contributory negligence, the success fee would be calculated on the basis of £375,000 rather than £750,00. This would mean a success fee of £20,000 + £27,500 = £47,500 rather than £66,250.

For employment appeal proceedings, the cap is a flat limit of 35% and for all other actions it is a flat limit of 50%.

Success fees are still not allowed in family actions – see section 5 of the 2018 Act and regulation 3 of the 2020 Regulations.

4.4 <u>Essential terms and conditions in a success fee agreement</u>

Regulation 4 of the 2020 Regulations provides as follows:

4.— Terms of a success fee agreement

(1) A success fee agreement must—

(a) include details of the matter, claim or proceedings, or parts thereof, to which the success fee agreement relates,

(b) specify the type of civil remedy which the recipient seeks,

(c) include a description of the work to be carried out by the provider,

(d) provide that in the event of a conflict with the provider's standard terms of engagement, the terms of the success fee agreement take precedence,

(e) specify the basis on which the amount of any fee potentially payable under the success fee agreement is to be determined,

(f) oblige the provider to consult with the recipient on any significant development including, but not limited to, the receipt of an offer of settlement,

(g) specify whether or not the provider intends to retain any expenses which are awarded to the recipient in civil proceedings or which it is agreed with another person that the recipient is entitled to recover[1],

(h) explain how to access the relevant procedure for dealing with complaints about the provider or providers,

(i) set out the circumstances in which the provider may, as a consequence of the recipient's conduct, terminate the agreement prior to the resolution of the matter to which it relates and require payment from the recipient for services provided prior to termination,

(j) provide that where the recipient terminates the success fee agreement prior to the resolution of the matter to which it relates, the recipient will normally be liable to pay for services provided prior to termination, and

(k) provide details of the fee which would be charged by the provider and any other sums which would be payable by the recipient to the provider, in the event that the provider or recipient terminates the agreement prior to the resolution of the matter to which it relates.

(2) If the success fee agreement provides that any fee potentially payable may be subject to change without further agreement, such as in the case of periodic increases to hourly rates charged by the provider, the success fee agreement must provide that changes will be notified to the recipient in writing as soon as reasonably practicable.

(3) In a matter that is, or could become, a claim for damages for personal injuries or the death of a person from personal injuries, the success fee agreement must provide that the provider is liable to pay where—

(a) a court makes an award of expenses in consequence of proceedings being conducted in the manner described in section 8(4)(a), (b) or (c) of the 2018 Act, and

(b) the court indicates that the conduct concerned was that of the provider and not the recipient.

The Law Society of Scotland provides an excellent template for such agreements that can be found on its website. It would be a brave or foolish solicitor who ignored the template.

It should be noted that these limits only apply to lawyers operating a success fee agreement. A claims manager is not so restricted. This may be important for bigger and riskier claims, where these limits could make it impossible to find backing. For example, clinical negligence actions routinely require a great deal of expensive investigation to ascertain whether they are viable. Even where supportive reports are obtained, the stringency of the *Hunter v Hanley* test mean that if the defenders find a responsible expert to contest liability, it is almost impossible to win. It may well be that for this type of case, pursuers will still need to find backing from claims managers, with the attendant loss of a bigger percentage of damages in the event of success. These are also the kind of case where legal aid is more likely to be relevant.

4.5 <u>Future losses and Periodical Payment Orders (PPOs)</u>

One of the most controversial and complicated aspects of the new regime is how to calculate the amount of a success fee that can be taken from future damages.

Section 6 of the 2018 Act provides as follows:

"**6 Personal injury claims**

(1) This section applies to a success fee agreement entered into in connection with a claim for damages for—

(a) personal injuries, or

(b) the death of a person from personal injuries.

(2) The agreement must provide that the recipient of the relevant services is not liable to make any payment (including outlays incurred in providing the services) to the provider in respect of the services, apart from the success fee, regardless of whether any damages are obtained.

(3) In subsection (2), *"outlays"* do not include any sums paid in respect of insurance premiums in connection with the claim to which the agreement relates.

(4) The agreement—

(a) may provide that any damages for future loss obtained in connection with the claim (the "future element") will be included in the amount of damages by reference to which the success fee is to, or may, be calculated (the "relevant amount of damages") if the future element is within subsection (5), but

(b) otherwise, must provide that any future element will not be included in the relevant amount of damages.

(5) The future element is within this subsection if it is to be paid in a lump sum and—

(a) does not exceed £1,000,000, or

(b) exceeds £1,000,000 and—

(i) the provider had not advised the recipient to accept that the future element be paid in periodical instalments, and

(ii) the condition in subsection (6) is met.

(6) The condition is—

(a) in the case where the damages are awarded by a court or tribunal, that the court or tribunal in awarding the future element has stated that it is satisfied that it is in the recipient's best interests that the future element be paid as a lump sum rather than in periodical instalments,

(b) in the case where the damages are obtained by agreement, that an independent actuary has, after having consulted the recipient personally in the absence of the provider, certified that in the actuary's view it is in the recipient's best interests that the future element be paid as a lump sum rather than in periodical instalments.

(7) The agreement is unenforceable to the extent that it makes provision contrary to subsection (2) or (4).

(8) The Scottish Ministers may by regulations substitute another sum for the sum for the time being specified in subsection (5)(a) and (b).

(9) In subsection (1), *personal injuries* include any disease and any impairment of a person's physical or mental condition.

(10) In subsection (6)(b), *actuary* means an Associate or Fellow of the Institute and Faculty of Actuaries

Put shortly, where future losses are awarded in the form of a PPO, they cannot be taken into account when calculating the success fee. This creates an immediate conflict of interest for the legal advisors, who have a financial interest in the claim being settled by way of a lump sum, whereas the pursuer will generally be better served by a PPO. This is partly because they will then not have to pay a success fee, but more fundamentally, it is the only way that they can ensure that they will receive damages for the whole of their lives.

This is because a lump sum will be calculated on the basis of a hypothetical life expectancy. In reality, even if that life expectancy is agreed between the experts, it is highly unlikely that the pursuer will live to that exact period. If the pursuer dies earlier, then there is a windfall to their estate. However, if they live beyond the predicted date, then they will run out of damages. Even if they do not live longer than expected, the risks of unexpected inflation, bad investments etc. make it far more sensible to take damages by way of a PPO.

In other words, it is going to be difficult to bring the exceptions in section 6(6) into play. The difficulty is compounded by the fact that it is unclear who will pay for the advice of the independent actuary. It is also difficult to see how the court will adjudicate on this, given that there is no equivalent of the Court of Protection in Scotland.

It is likely that this provision will give rise to significant practical difficulties.

CHAPTER FIVE

QUALIFIED ONE-WAY COSTS SHIFTING (QOCS)

5.1 Introduction

The risk of an adverse finding in expenses is a significant disincentive to litigation. It is a particularly powerful disincentive where one party has significantly deeper pockets than the other, which is the standard scenario in personal injuries litigation, where the defender is usually a public body or backed by an insurer. QOCS is an exception to the general rule that the successful party is able to recover at least some of their expenses from the other side. It should be noted that the exception applies in all personal injury litigation, regardless of the financial resources of the defender, subject only to the qualifications discussed below.

Section 8 of the 2018 Act provides as follows:

"**8 Restriction on pursuer's liability for expenses in personal injury claims**

(1) This section applies in civil proceedings where—

(a) the person bringing the proceedings makes a claim for damages for—

(i) personal injuries, or

(ii) the death of a person from personal injuries, and

(b) the person conducts the proceedings in an appropriate manner.

(2) The court must not make an award of expenses against the person in respect of any expenses which relate to—

(a) the claim, or

(b) any appeal in respect of the claim.

(3) Subsection (2) does not prevent the court from making an award in respect of expenses which relate to any other type of claim in the proceedings.

(4) For the purposes of subsection (1)(b), a person conducts civil proceedings in an appropriate manner unless the person or the person's legal representative—

(a) makes a fraudulent representation or otherwise acts fraudulently in connection with the claim or proceedings,

(b) behaves in a manner which is manifestly unreasonable in connection with the claim or proceedings, or

(c) otherwise, conducts the proceedings in a manner that the court considers amounts to an abuse of process.

(5) For the purpose of subsection (4)(a), the standard of proof is the balance of probabilities.

(6) Subsection (2) is subject to any exceptions that may be specified in an act of sederunt under section 103(1) or 104(1) of the Courts Reform (Scotland) Act 2014.

(7) In subsection (1)(a), *personal injuries* include any disease and any impairment of a person's physical or mental condition."

QOCS was finally brought into force by the Act of Sederunt (Rules of the Court of Session 1994, Sheriff Appeal Court Rules and Sheriff

Court Rules Amendment) (Qualified One-Way Costs Shifting) 2021. Section 2 provides that the new rules apply to first instance proceedings commenced on or after 30th June 2021, and to any appeals arising from first instance proceedings commenced on or after the same date.

The new rules for the Court of Session are as follows:

"CHAPTER 41B QUALIFIED ONE-WAY COSTS SHIFTING

41B.1.— Application and interpretation of this Chapter

(1) This Chapter applies in civil proceedings, where either or both—

(a) an application for an award of expenses is made to the court;

(b) such an award is made by the court.

(2) Where this Chapter applies—

(a) rules 29.1(2) and (3) (abandonment of actions), 40.15(6) (appeals deemed abandoned) and 41.17(3)(b) (procedure on abandonment);

(b) any common law rule entitling a pursuer to abandon an action or an appeal, to the extent that it concerns expenses,

are disapplied.

(3) In this Chapter—

"the Act" means the Civil Litigation (Expenses and Group Proceedings) (Scotland) Act 2018;

"the applicant" has the meaning given in rule 41B.2(1), and *"applicants"* is construed accordingly;

"civil proceedings" means civil proceedings to which section 8 of the Act (restriction on pursuer's liability for expenses in personal injury claims) applies.

41B.2.— Application for an award of expenses

(1) Where civil proceedings have been brought by a pursuer, another party to the action ("the applicant") may make an application to the court for an award of expenses to be made against the pursuer, on one or more of the grounds specified in either or both—

(a) section 8(4)(a) to (c) of the Act;

(b) paragraph (2) of this rule.

(2) The grounds specified in this paragraph, which are exceptions to section 8(2) of the Act, are as follows—

(a) failure by the pursuer to obtain an award of damages greater than the sum offered by way of a tender lodged in process;

(b) unreasonable delay on the part of the pursuer in accepting a sum offered by way of a tender lodged in process;

(c) abandonment of the action or the appeal by the pursuer in terms of rules 29.1(1), 40.15(1) or 41.15(1), or at common law.

41B.3.— Award of expenses

(1) Subject to paragraph (2), the determination of an application made under rule 41B.2(1) is at the discretion of the court.

(2) Where, having determined an application made under rule 41B.2(1), the court makes an award of expenses against the pursuer on the ground specified in rule 41B.2(2)(a) or (b)—

(a) the pursuer's liability is not to exceed the amount of expenses the applicant has incurred after the date of the tender;

(b) the liability of the pursuer to the applicant, or applicants, who lodged the tender is to be limited to an aggregate sum, payable to all applicants (if more than one) of 75% of the amount of damages awarded to the pursuer, and that sum is to be calculated without offsetting against those expenses any expenses due to the pursuer by the applicant, or applicants, before the date of the tender;

(c) the court must order that the pursuer's liability is not to exceed the sum referred to in sub-paragraph (b), notwithstanding that any sum assessed by the Auditor of Court as payable under the tender procedure may be greater or, if modifying the expenses in terms of rule 42.5 (modification or disallowance of expenses)[6] or 42.6(1) (modification of expenses awarded against assisted persons), that such modification does not exceed that referred to in sub-paragraph (b);

(d) where the award of expenses is in favour of more than one applicant the court, failing agreement between the applicants, is to apportion the award of expenses recoverable under the tender procedure between them.

(3) Where, having determined an application made under rule 41B.2(1), the court makes an award of expenses against the pursuer on the ground specified in rule 41B.2(2)(c), the court may make such orders in respect of expenses, as it considers appropriate, including—

(a) making an award of decree of dismissal dependant on payment of expenses by the pursuer within a specified period of time;

(b) provision for the consequences of failure to comply with any conditions applied by the court.

41B.4.— Procedure

(1) An application under rule 41B.2(1)—

(a) must be made by motion, in writing, and Chapter 23 (motions)[7] otherwise applies to motions made under this Chapter;

(b) may be made at any stage in the case prior to the pronouncing of an interlocutor disposing of the expenses of the action or, as the case may be, the appeal.

(2) Where an application under rule 41B.2(1) is made, the court may make such orders as it thinks fit for dealing with the application, including an order—

(a) requiring the applicant to intimate the application to any other person;

(b) requiring any party to lodge a written response;

(c) requiring the lodging of any document;

(d) fixing a hearing.

41B.5. Award against legal representatives

Section 8(2) of the Act does not prevent the court from making an award of expenses against a pursuer's legal representative in terms of section 11 (awards of expenses against legal representatives) of the Act."

Similar provisions apply in the Sheriff Court and the Sheriff Appeal Court.

5.2 The costs shifting is one-way

The first key element of QOCS is that this is a one-way restriction. The successful pursuer can still recover their judicial expenses, including an additional fee where appropriate. It is only the successful defender who cannot recover.

Although concerns have been expressed that this will lead to hopeless or speculative claims being raised in the hope of achieving a nuisance value settlement, it is important to remember that there are significant legal expenses in raising a court action. These include the costs of the lawyers but also experts and court dues. Someone is at risk for these costs, whether it be the lawyers, an insurer, a claims manager or the pursuer themselves. In other words there are still significant disincentives to raising actions that are likely to be defended successfully. Losing a court case will still have significant consequences for the pursuer, or at least for their legal representatives. Since it is the lawyers who are best placed to determine the prospects of success, that seems a reasonable position.

The difficulty arises with the dishonest claimant who lies about some fundamental aspect of the claim, whether that be in relation to liability or quantum. There are limits to how far a lawyer can distrust his own client. It is not possible to obtain surveillance videos of the client to test their evidence. For this reason it is standard practice to include a condition in the terms of business that the lawyer will not act "no win, no fee" in the event that the client is found to have been dishonest. It is also important to establish with the client that they will be liable not only for their own expenses but also the other side's in such an event.

5.3 The costs shifting is qualified

The really interesting questions arise around when an unsuccessful pursuer will lose the protection of QOCS. Section 8(4) provides 3 exceptions to the general rule that the pursuer will not have to pay the successful defenders' expenses. The first is, not surprisingly, where the pursuer (or their lawyer) has acted fraudulently. The third is where there has been an abuse of process. The second, and the most general, exception is 8(4)(b) which engages when the pursuer acts in a way that is "manifestly unreasonable".

On the face of it, acting fraudulently or in a way that amounts to an abuse of process will automatically amount to manifestly unreasonable behaviour, so it is not entirely clear why a defender would rely on 8(4)(a) or (c). Accordingly, it seems likely that the cases will mostly focus on 8(4)(b). However, it may well be that the seriousness of the other 2 exceptions will give some content to the degree of unreasonableness required to engage 8(4)(b).

It is certainly clear that the courts will be looking for "Wednesbury" unreasonableness, that is to say, an act so unreasonable that no reasonable authority could endorse it (*Associated Provincial Picture Houses Ltd v Wednesbury Corp* [1948] 1 KB 223 at 230: "it must be proved to be unreasonable in the sense that the court considers it to be a decision that no reasonable body could have come to"). This is apparent from the Stage 1 Report of the Justice Committee on the Bill for the 2018 Act:

"Section 8(4) of the Bill provides for three circumstances in which a pursuer will be considered not to have conducted proceedings appropriately and therefore lose QOCS protection. The Committee heard from pursuer, defender and insurer representatives that the tests set out in the Bill were insufficiently clear and would result in satellite litigation...

"The Committee heard a range of concerns about the drafting of section 8(4) of the Bill, which sets out the circumstances in which a pursuer will lose the protection of qualified one-way costs shifting (QOCS). The Committee therefore welcomes the Scottish Government's commitment to amend this provision to ensure greater clarity.

"The Committee asks the Scottish Government to ensure that these amendments properly reflect Sheriff Principal Taylor's recommendations and take into account his suggestions in oral evidence to the Committee as to how sections 8(4)(a) and 8(4)(b) should be drafted. This includes amending section 8(4)(b) to reflect the test of Wednesbury unreasonableness. The Committee also notes the suggestion made by the Forum of Insurance Lawyers that the test in section 8(4)(a) should relate to claims rather than proceedings, in order to cover the majority of claims which are never litigated in court."

In general, satisfying such a high test requires clear and cogent evidence. As Lord Hoffman said in *Secretary of State for the Home Department v Rehman* [2003] 1 AC 153, 194 (my emphasis added): "The civil standard of proof always means more likely than not. The only higher degree of probability required by the law is the criminal standard. But, as Lord Nicholls of Birkenhead explained in *In re H (Minors) (Sexual Abuse: Standard of Proof)* [1996] AC 563, 586, some things are inherently more likely than others. It would need more cogent evidence to satisfy one that the creature seen walking in Regent's Park was more likely than not to have been a lioness than to be satisfied to the same standard of probability that it was an Alsatian. **On this basis, cogent evidence is generally required to satisfy a civil tribunal that a person has been fraudulent or behaved in some other reprehensible manner.** But the question is always whether the tribunal thinks it more probable than not."

A degree of exaggeration is not unusual in personal injury litigation, particularly when a litigant is trying to persuade a medical expert employed by the other side that their complaints are genuine. Furthermore, courts are well aware of the fallibility of human memory and the fact that everyone can remember an event in a way that is inconsistent with objective evidence. See the oft-quoted analysis of Leggat J (as he then was) in *Gestmin v Credit Suisse* [2013] EWHC 3560 (Comm).

The most difficult clients are those who have clearly convinced themselves of facts that simply cannot be proven. An entirely credible witness can prove to be unreliable. The key question will be when that conduct crosses the boundary and becomes manifestly unreasonable or, to use the English test, fundamentally dishonest.

5.4 <u>Abandoned actions</u>

What can a pursuer's legal team do if it becomes apparent that the pursuer has acted in a manifestly unreasonable way, or committed an act of fraud, or acted in a way that amounts to an abuse of process? The obvious answer is to bale out of the claim at the first opportunity. That will limit the damage but is unlikely to prevent the defenders from successfully arguing for the removal of QOCS protection.

In *Rouse v Aviva Insurance Ltd* [15/1/16] Bradford County Court held that in such cases, there may need to be a hearing purely on the question of fundamental dishonesty. See also the case of *Kite v*

Phoenix Pub Group, where the claimant was not allowed to abandon his claim, the defendants moved to have the case struck out and the protection of QOCS was lost.

RCS RCS 41B.2.(2)(c) specifically provides that the court may make an award of expenses in favour of a defender against whom the pursuer has abandoned their claim. It is not difficult to see that such decisions will be difficult to make on the motion roll, unless parties can agree the basic facts, and that there may be occasion on which the court will need to hear evidence. Alternatively, the courts may be prepared to determine the matter on the basis of *ex parte* statements of counsel, as is common in procedure roll debates on time-bar (see the observations of the court in *Clark v Mclean* 1994 SC 410 at 413).

Thompson v Go North East Ltd [30/8/16] Sunderland CC went even further, including a wasted costs order against the solicitors after the claimant had attempted to abandon a fundamentally dishonest claim. It is important to remember that section 11 of the 2018 Act specifically provides the court with the power to make an award against the legal representative where there has been "a serious breach" of that lawyer's duties to the court.

Put shortly, abandoning a claim is not necessarily an easy escape route where a claim goes off the rails and all involved should be aware of that.

5.5 Multiple defenders

What happens where the pursuer is successful against one defender but not against another?

In *Cartwright v Venduct Engineering Ltd* [2018] 1 WLR 6137 the claimant sued 6 defendants for Noise Induced Hearing Loss. He was settled the claim against the fourth to sixth defendants for £20,000 but was not successful against the first to third defendants. The third defendants sought an award of expenses out of the principal sum paid by the fourth to sixth defendants. It was held that in principle this was acceptable. However, that case turned on very different rules of procedure in England and Wales.

In the Court of Session the position would be determined by RCS 41B.2.(2)(c) (see above). No doubt the fact that the pursuer had obtained damages from another defender would be a factor for the court to consider in exercising its discretion as to whether expenses should be awarded against the pursuer.

5.6 <u>Counter claims</u>

A is driving along a single carriageway country road and takes a blind bend. He collides head on with B coming in the opposite direction. Each claims that the other was on the wrong side of the road.

A sues B and B counter claims. A is unsuccessful and it is held that he was solely at fault. B is successful in his counterclaim. Can he recover his expenses or will A be able to claim QOCS protection, on the basis that he was an unsuccessful pursuer? Does it matter if B initially sues A and A counter claims? What if A is very seriously injured but B only suffers minor injuries? What if both are equally to blame – do they both get QOCS protections, so that neither insurer has to pay the expenses?

Some of these questions have been posed in cases south of the border and contradictory answers have been given.

In *Ketchion v McEwan* (2018, Newcastle County Court) the claimant sued for financial losses arising from a road traffic accident. He had not suffered any personal injury and so there was no question of QOCS protection applying to his claim. The defendant counter-claimed for personal injuries sustained in the same accident.

32

The counter claim was unsuccessful, but the defendant argued that he was entitled to QOCS protection. On appeal, it was held that he was entitled to such protection in relation to the whole proceedings.

This decision caused some concern to practitioners for fear that it would encourage spurious counter claims. Under the Scottish provisions, that fear is probably unfounded as such a counter claim could easily be seen as manifestly unreasonable, or possibly even an abuse of process.

In *Waring v McDonnell* (2018, Brighton County Court) 2 cyclists collided head on with each other, causing personal injuries to both. Waring sued McDonnell and McDonnell counterclaimed. Waring was successful and McDonnell claimed QOCS protection on the basis of the *Ketchion* decision. However, the court denied him that protection on the basis that he was deemed to be an unsuccessful defendant rather than unsuccessful claimant. Would the same result have obtained if McDonnell had sued first? In that case it could have been said that he was the unsuccessful claimant.

Presumably the test must be one of substance rather than form. That might be easy where one party is clearly more at fault, or suffers significantly more serious injuries, but what if both could reasonably be characterized as a pursuer rather than a defender? Section 8(2) of the 2018 Act is mandatory in its terms and the 2021 regulations do not allow the court any discretion beyond the limited exceptions in section 8(4) of the 2018 Act or 41.B.2(2).

CHAPTER SIX

QOCS CASES IN ENGLAND
AND WALES

6.1 Introduction

Given that QOCS has been in existence south of the border for a
number of years, it would make sense to look at the case law in that
jurisdiction to see how a court in Scotland might approach the same
issues. However, it has to be recognised at the outset that the
wording of the provisions in England is very different.

Chapter 44 of the Civil Procedure Rules deals with QOCS in
general and Rule 44.16 provides that "Orders for costs made against
the claimant may be enforced to the full extent of such orders with
the permission of the court where the claim is found on the balance
of probabilities to be fundamentally dishonest". The concept of
fundamental dishonesty does not feature at all in Scottish legislation.

The second important caveat when looking at the cases south of the
border is that there appears to be a far greater incidence of outright
fraudulent claims in England and Wales. This has led to a far more
jaundiced approach from the judiciary than one would expect from a
Scottish court. For example, in *Molodi v Cambridge Vibration
Maintenance Service* [2018] RTR 25 the High Court stated at para
[44] that "The problem of fraudulent and exaggerated whiplash
claims is well recognised and should, in my judgment, cause judges
in the county court to approach such claims with a degree of
caution, if not suspicion." It is difficult to imagine a Scottish court
suggesting that any case should be approached with anything other
than a completely open mind.

6.2 *Ivey v Genting Casinos* [2018] AC 381

Although this was not a case concerning QOCS or even expenses more generally, it is authoritative guidance on what amounts to a dishonest state of mind

The claimant was a professional gambler who won £7.7m by a system known as edge sorting – a form of card counting based on the design irregularities on the back of playing cards. The defendant, which had not known about edge-sorting, refused to pay the claimant his winnings on the ground that such play altered the odds against it unfairly. The claimant brought an action for recovery of the sums which he had won. The defendant contended, inter alia, that the gaming contract between the parties had an implied term that the claimant would not cheat or otherwise act to defeat the essential premise of the game and if he did so the contract would be void and he would recover no winnings under it, which term he had broken.

The question arose as to whether the appellant's genuine subjective belief that what he was doing was not dishonest was sufficient, or whether an objective approach should apply.

The Supreme Court held that there was a two-stage test, the first being subjective and the second objective. The first step is to ascertain, subjectively, the actual state of the individual's knowledge or belief as to the facts. The reasonableness of that belief was a matter of evidence going to whether they had held the belief, but it was not an additional requirement that the belief had to be reasonable; the question was whether it was genuinely held. When the state of mind was established, the question whether the conduct was honest or dishonest was to be determined by applying the objective standards of ordinary decent people. There was no requirement that the defendant must appreciate that the conduct was dishonest by those standards. Per Lord Hughes at para [62]:

> *"Although a dishonest state of mind is a subjective mental state, the standard by which the law determines whether it is dishonest is objective. If by ordinary standards a defendant's mental state would be characterised as dishonest, it is irrelevant that the defendant judges by different standards. The Court of Appeal held this to be the correct state of the law and their Lordships agree."*

It seems likely that this case will be of interest to Scottish courts in the same way that it has been in England and Wales.

6.3 "Fundamental dishonesty"

One of the first cases in England to discuss the level of misconduct required to demonstrate fundamental dishonesty was *Gosling v Hailo and another* 2014 WL 3002771 (Judge Moloney QC, 29th April 2014, Cambridge County Court).

The claimant suffered serious injury to knee involving ladder manufactured by D1 and sold by D2. Due to an exaggerated care claim, a costs order was made against the claimant. The claim was for £80,000 but settled before trial for £5,000 following surveillance evidence described by the judge as "frankly devastating". It was held that to be considered fundamental, the dishonesty would have to go to the root or a substantial part of the claim and not merely some collateral matter or minor, self-contained head of damage. However, it was not necessary for the dishonesty to go to the whole of either liability or quantum. The purpose of the provision is to test whether the claimant was "deserving" of costs (expenses) protection.

Although this is only a decision at County Court level, the following passages in the judgment have recently been approved by the Court of Appeal in *Howlett v Davies* 2018 1 WLR 948 at para 17:

> *"44. It appears to me that this phrase in the rules has to be interpreted purposively and contextually in the light of the context.*

This is, of course, the determination of whether the claimant is "deserving", as Jackson LJ put it, of the protection (from the costs liability that would otherwise fall on him) extended, for reasons of social policy, by the QOCS rules. It appears to me that when one looks at the matter in that way, one sees that what the rules are doing is distinguishing between two levels of dishonesty: dishonesty in relation to the claim which is not fundamental so as to expose such a claimant to costs liability, and dishonesty which is fundamental, so as to give rise to costs liability.

45. The corollary term to "fundamental" would be a word with some such meaning as "incidental" or "collateral". Thus, a claimant should not be exposed to costs liability merely because he is shown to have been dishonest as to some collateral matter or perhaps as to some minor, self-contained head of damage. If, on the other hand, the dishonesty went to the root of either the whole of his claim or a substantial part of his claim, then it appears to me that it would be a fundamentally dishonest claim: a claim which depended as to a substantial or important part of itself upon dishonesty."

6.4 Illustrative cases

Zimi v London Central Bus Company [8/1/15] Central London CC

The claim was based on an allegation that the defendant's bus collided with the claimant's car. The judge viewed CCTV footage and held that there was no collision and that the claimant could not have honestly believed that there was a collision of the kind claimed. Accordingly, the claimant was ordered to pay full costs.

Zurich Insurance plc v Bain [4/6/15] Newcastle CC

Low speed RTA in which liability was admitted and vehicle repairs paid. The claimant made a claim for a back injury that was held to be entirely fabricated. The district judge surprisingly refused to make a costs order against the claimant. On appeal it was held that this went beyond mere exaggeration or embellishment and the whole basis of the claim was fundamentally dishonest: "*it props up, and provides the sole basis for the claim*".

James v Diamanttek [8/2/16] Coventry County Court

Claim for noise induced hearing loss. The claimant initially alleged that no hearing protection was provided until the last two years of his employment, but later conceded that he had been provided with hearing protection post 2006. The judge concluded that the claimant had not been telling the truth at the hearing, rejected his claim and made a costs order against him. Although the district judge did not hold this to amount to fundamental dishonesty, the defendants were successful on appeal. Having found that the claimant was not at any time during his employment deprived of hearing protection as he had alleged, she could not justifiably have concluded that the claim was not fundamentally dishonest. The crucial finding was that he was not telling the truth – he was incredible rather than merely unreliable.

Meadows v La Tasca [2016] 6 WLUK 407

In a slipping case, the district judge held the evidence of the claimant and her supporting witness to be "riddled with inconsistencies" and so removed QOCS protection. On appeal, the judge held that plain inconsistencies in the evidence did not amount to fundamental dishonesty. At paragraph 18, the judge made the following interesting distinction:

"If a lie is told merely to bolster an honest claim or defence, then that will not necessarily tell against the liar. But if the lie goes to the whole root of the claim or defence, then it may well indicate that the claim or defence (as the case may be) is itself fundamentally dishonest."11.

Nesham v Sunrich Clothing Ltd [2016] 4 WLUK 506

RTA in which the claimant failed to establish liability because the judge did not accept his version of events. However, this did not amount to fundamental dishonesty.

Menary v Darnton [30/1/17] 12 WLUK 308

The court held that the claim rather than the claimant must be dishonest. Where it was held that the alleged accident had not actually happened, it was easy to say that there was fundamental dishonesty.

> *"11. The use of the word 'dishonesty' in the present context necessarily imports well understood and ordinary concepts of deceit, falsity and deception. In essence, it is the advancing of a claim without an honest and genuine belief in its truth. [F]or present purposes, fundamental dishonesty may be taken to be some deceit that goes to the root of the claim. The purpose of the phrase is twofold: first, to distinguish any dishonesty from the exaggerations, concealments and the like that accompany personal injury claims from time to time. Such exaggerations, concealment and so forth may be dishonest, but they cannot sensibly be said to be fundamentally dishonest; they do not go to the root of the claim. Second, the fundamental dishonesty is related to the claim not to the claimant. This must be deliberate on the part of those who drafted the Civil Procedure Rules. It is the claim the defendant has been obliged to meet, and if that claim has been tainted by fundamental dishonesty, then in fairness, and in justice and in*

accordance with the overriding objective, the defendant should be able to recover the costs incurred in meeting an action that was proved, on balance, to be fundamentally dishonest."

...

36. I return therefore to the question of whether or not this claim was fundamentally dishonest. I am satisfied beyond any doubt that it was. The deputy district judge found that there was no impact. There was therefore no road traffic accident, no damage to the car caused and no consequential injuries to the claimant. The documents subsequently produced were indirectly manufactured by the claimant in pursuit of a claim that had no basis in fact or reality. This was not a case of some exaggeration of loss or symptom, nor a case of inventing an additional head of damage in an otherwise legitimate claim. There was no honest claim here"

O'Brien v Royal Mail Group 20/5/18 QBD (Manchester)
[2019] 5 WLUK 646

The claimant alleged that the defendant had driven into the back of his van at high speed, causing physical injuries that caused him to attend hospital, to be off work for 6 weeks and to suffer restriction in activities for 8 months. The defendant contended that the impact was at very low speed and that the claimant had not suffered any injury. The judge at first instance held that the impact was no more than 5mph and that the claimant had suffered no personal injury. However, she found that he was not fundamentally dishonest. On appeal, it was held that this finding was contrary to the evidence and that QOCS protection should be disapplied.

Keane v Tollafield [8/8/18] Birmingham County Court
[2018] 8 WLUK 30

This was a clinical negligence claim in which the claimant alleged that she had not given properly informed consent to surgery. Her oral evidence contradicted her written statement in certain respects. Her claim failed but the judge held that she was unreliable rather than incredible and that QOCS protection should apply. The judgment contains an interesting analysis of the fallibility of the human memory under reference to the dicta of Leggat J (as he then was) in the case of *Gestmin v Credit Suisse* [2013] EWHC 3560 (Comm).

Haidar v DSM Demolition [2019] EWHC 2712 (QB)

The claimant was driving a taxi which he stopped suddenly and the defendant ran into the back of him. The claimant sued the defendant for personal injuries and also credit hire charges amounting to some £30,000. His claim failed and it came out in the trial that he had falsely denied having a credit card, which meant that he did not have to resort to credit hire (see *Lagden v O'Connor*). On appeal, it was held that he had been fundamentally dishonest and so the QOCS protection was disapplied.

The *Ivey v Genting Casinos UK Ltd* approach (see above), involving a two-stage test for dishonesty, so that an unreasonable subjective belief will not be sufficient, is clearly illustrated in the case of *Brint v Barking, Havering and Redbridge University Hospitals NHS Trust* [2021] EWHC 290 (QB):

> *"102. This has been an extremely complex case. However, when I stand back and look at the totality of the evidence I am far from persuaded that the claimant has deliberately made up events that did not occur or that she has deliberately told lies about her condition in order to advance her claim. Applying the two-stage*

test [in Ivey], I am satisfied that the claimant genuinely believed in the truth of the evidence that she gave and that, applying the standards of ordinary decent people I find as a fact that although her evidence was wholly unreliable in the sense that I do not accept it, she has not been dishonest. I therefore reject the allegation of fundamental dishonesty."

6.5 Claims involving an element of personal injury

QOCS are likely to cover professional negligence claims that include an element of mental or physical injury. In *Walkin v South Manchester Health Authority* [1995] WLR 1543 the plaintiff sought damages for personal injuries and consequential losses following on from a failed sterilisation. The action was raised outwith the triennium and the defendant health authority pled a defence of time-bar. The plaintiff tried to argue that her claim did not consist of or include a claim for damages in respect of personal injuries but merely damages in respect of the additional cost to the plaintiff of bringing up a child. The Court of Appeal disagreed and held that a claim for damages arising from a failed sterilisation operation which resulted in an unwanted pregnancy and the birth of a healthy child was a claim for "damages in respect of personal injuries" within the meaning of section 11(1) of the Limitation Act 1980, howsoever pleaded; that claims in such circumstances for pre-natal pain and suffering and post-natal economic costs arose out of the same cause of action; that the unwanted conception, whether caused by negligent advice or negligent surgery, was a personal injury in the sense of an "impairment" within the meaning of section 38(1) of the Act of 1980 which arose at the moment of conception; and that, accordingly, the plaintiff's claim was statute-barred. On this reasoning, such a claim would qualify for QOCS protection.

However, the protection will only extend to that part of the claim, not the whole action. In *Jeffreys v Commissioner of the Police for the*

Metropolis [2017] EWHC 1505 (QB) the claimant brought a claim against the police for damages, including aggravated and exemplary damages, for assault, false imprisonment, misfeasance in public office and malicious prosecution. He alleged that the police had provided concocted evidence to the Crown Prosecution Service. He claimed that he had suffered pain, distress, anxiety and loss of liberty, and specifically alleged that he had suffered soft tissue injuries to his hands, and that the police's actions had exacerbated his paranoid schizophrenia. After an eight-day jury trial, his claim was dismissed. At a separate costs hearing, the trial judge accepted that QOCS applied; he rejected the police's argument that the claim had been fundamentally dishonest, which would have provided an exception to QOWCS under CPR r.44.16(1), but he found that the exception in r.44.16(2)(b) applied, because at the heart of the claim were allegations of misfeasance, and the personal injury aspects of the claim were ancillary. He ordered the claimant to pay the police's costs of the action, and permitted the police to enforce that costs order to the extent of 70%. The Court of Appeal dismissed the claimant's appeal.

A slightly different approach was taken in *Roberts v Kesson* [2020] EWHC 521 (QB), a case under section 57 of the Criminal Justice and Courts Act 2015 (see further below). That case related to an RTA after which the claimant sought *inter alia* replacement cost of vehicle at £10,400 in addition to a claim for personal injuries. In fact the vehicle had been successfully repaired. The rest of the claim was only worth about £4,000. The court held that the dishonest claim had to be assessed globally against the entire claim, having regard to its particular importance. Applying that holistic approach, the claimant's dishonest claim was fundamental. It was not minor or peripheral. A finding of fundamental dishonesty on that claim should have been made by the recorder and the action should have been dismissed. Obviously, it is not possible to take a "divided success" approach to the binary question of whether a case should be dismissed or not, as opposed to a finding of expenses where there is ample scope for compromise.

Once again the decisions in England and Wales have to be treated with caution as much turned on the particular wording of the relevant procedural rules. However, section 8 of the 2018 Act is equally ambiguous as to whether "the claim" is divisible or not.

6.6 Section 57 of the Criminal Justice and Courts Act 2015

Some further guidance on the degree of dishonesty that the courts see as going beyond acceptable can be found in the caselaw relating to this provision that only applies in England and Wales. It is the provision that allows an otherwise valid claim to be dismissed purely on the grounds that some part of it is tainted by "fundamental dishonesty". The section provides as follows:

> (1) This section applies where, in proceedings on a claim for damages in respect of personal injury ("the primary claim")—
>
> — the court finds that the claimant is entitled to damages in respect of the claim, but
>
> — on an application by the defendant for the dismissal of the claim under this section, the court is satisfied on the balance of probabilities that the claimant has been fundamentally dishonest in relation to the primary claim or a related claim.
>
> (2) The court must dismiss the primary claim, unless it is satisfied that the claimant would suffer substantial injustice if the claim were dismissed.

(3) The duty under subsection (2) includes the dismissal of any element of the primary claim in respect of which the claimant has not been dishonest.

(4) The court's order dismissing the claim must record the amount of damages that the court would have awarded to the claimant in respect of the primary claim but for the dismissal of the claim.

(5) When assessing costs in the proceedings, a court which dismisses a claim under this section must deduct the amount recorded in accordance with subsection (4) from the amount which it would otherwise order the claimant to pay in respect of costs incurred by the defendant.

Although the same wording is used for the test under section 57 as for the test for QOCS in England and Wales, one might expect a higher standard to apply under section 57. It is one thing to deprive a claimant of QOCS protection where the alleged accident did not occur at all. It is quite another to deprive a claimant of a claim in which they have suffered injury, sometimes quite serious, as the result of admitted negligence of another. In practice there does not seem to be any distinction between the two tests.

The leading authority is *London Organising Committee of the Olympic and Paralympic Games (In Liquidation) v Sinfield* [2018] PIQR P8. In that case, the claimant had broken his left arm and wrist while acting as an assistant to spectators at the 2012 Olympic and Paralympic Games. The defendants admitted liability. Among the special damages claimed was a claim for gardening expenses. The claimant alleged that the accident had caused him to employ a gardener to look after his two-acre garden, a task which he and his wife had previously carried out. The total claimed, including for future gardening expenses, was just short of £14,000. That represented roughly 42% of the special damages sought and about

28% of the total claim for special and general damages (the latter were agreed at £16,000). The claimant's list of documents referred to invoices from the gardener said to have been engaged. However, it transpired that the gardener had been working for the respondent and his wife since 2005, that his work did not change as a result of the accident and resultant injuries, that the invoices did not come from him and that what the claimant had said about having to employ a gardener because of the accident was not true. The defendants sought the dismissal of the claim under section 57 on the basis that the claimant had been fundamentally dishonest in relation to it. The judge rejected that application, finding that the claimant had not been dishonest, but rather "muddled, confused and careless", in relation to the preliminary schedule of damages; that he had been dishonest in creating false invoices and in stating in his witness statement that the accident had caused him to employ a gardener for the first time; that the dishonesty did not contaminate the entire claim; that there was a genuine claim for personal injuries which "went wrong" when the claimant was careless and then dishonest; that the claimant had not been fundamentally dishonest, but if he had been it would be substantially unjust for the entire claim to be dismissed when the dishonesty related to a peripheral part of the claim and the remainder of it was genuine.

The defendants appealed and were successful. It was held that a claimant should be found to be fundamentally dishonest if the defendant proved on a balance of probabilities that the claimant had acted dishonestly in relation to the primary claim and/or a related claim (as defined in section 57(8)), and that he had substantially affected the presentation of his case, in respect of either liability or quantum, in a way which potentially adversely affected the defendant in a significant way, judged in the context of the particular facts and circumstances of the litigation. Dishonesty was to be judged according to the test set out by the Supreme Court in *Ivey v Genting Casinos UK Ltd* (see above). If the judge was so satisfied, he had to dismiss the claim, including any element of the primary claim in respect of which the claimant had not been dishonest, unless, in accordance with section 57(2), he was satisfied that the claimant would suffer substantial injustice. "Substantial injustice" had to mean more than the mere fact that the claimant would lose his damages for those heads of claim that were not tainted with dishonesty. What would generally be required was some substantial injustice arising as a consequence of the loss of those damages (see paras 62, 64-65 of judgment).

Applying that approach to the facts of this case, the judge had been wrong to find that the respondent had been merely muddled and careless in relation to the preliminary schedule of damages. The schedule contained dishonest misstatements. However, even on the judge's findings what the claimant did was fundamentally dishonest. He presented a claim for special damages in a significant sum, and the judge found that the largest head of damage was evidenced by the dishonest creation of false invoices and by a dishonest witness statement. Both pieces of dishonesty were premeditated and maintained over many months until the true picture was uncovered. The claimant presented his case on quantum in a dishonest way which could have resulted in the appellant paying out far more than it could properly, on honest evidence, have been ordered to do after a trial. Further, the judge made no findings capable of supporting a conclusion that if the whole claim was dismissed it would result in substantial injustice to the respondent.

Matthewson v Crump [2020] EWHC 3167 (QB)

This is an interesting case that seems to analyse dishonesty in purely subjective terms. The judge held that the claimant had failed on the merits in any event, but went on to deal with the question of whether he would have dismissed the claim under section 57 otherwise:

"101. In order to establish that the Claimant has pursued a "fundamentally dishonest" claim, it must be shown there was dishonesty which goes to the root or heart of the claim, or to a part of it. Dishonesty which is merely incidental or collateral to the claim will not suffice. Dishonesty for these purposes is subjective. It does not matter if the Claimant was unreasonable in believing in the veracity of his claim. Provided he genuinely believed in the veracity of all the core aspects of his claim, it will not be fundamentally dishonest. In essence a claim will be dishonest if the person putting it forward does not believe that some core aspect of it (whether concerned with liability or quantum) is true."

It is not clear that this approach is consistent with *Ivey v Genting Casinos* (see above).

An interesting feature of section 57 is that the courts appear to have become increasingly bold in its application. At first it was quite difficult to find reported cases but in recent years there have been a number of examples.

An unusual case was *Patel v Arriva Midlands Ltd* [2019] P.I.Q.R. P13. The claimant was involved in an RTA and suffered cardiac arrest and brain haemorrhage. Liability was admitted. When examined by medical experts for both sides, the claimant was unresponsive, although the experts were unable to explain the extent of the claimed disability. The defendants carried out surveillance and video evidence showed the claimant out and about. The defendants moved to have the claim dismissed before the trial on quantum. The claimant simply failed to respond to the evidence and did not attend the motion. Unsurprisingly, the motion was granted.

Less clear-cut cases include *Garroway v Holland & Barrett* [2020] 3 WLUK 582 where the claimant was injured at work when she walked into a partially lowered shutter. The claim was for facial and spinal injuries. The spinal injuries were held to be fabricated and the facial injuries were only worth £650. The claim was dismissed for fundamental dishonesty.

In *Iddon v Warner* [2021] 3 WLUK 432 the claimant sought damages of £900,000 for serious functional disability caused by a delayed diagnosis of breast cancer leading to mastectomy and chemotherapy that should have been avoided. However, evidence showed she was still able to compete in open water swimming events and the claim was dismissed on the basis of fundamental dishonesty. But for the dismissal of her claim, she would have been awarded £70,050.32.

In *Hogarth v Marstons* [2021] 3 WLUK 229 a 14-year old slipped on grease at the defendants' premises. She sued the occupiers for £6,250 in general damages and £91.15 in special damages. Liability was established, subject to 50% contributory negligence. However, it was held that the claimant had lied about going to hospital after the accident and so the action was dismissed. But for s57, award would have been £2,300 less 50%.

Another example is *Smith v Haringey LBC* [2021] EWHC 615 (QB). There the claimant suffered a back injury at work and was liability admitted, subject to deduction of 25%. The claimant had suffered back pain before the accident but failed to disclose it. In my experience this is common in back injury claims and indeed it is probably unusual to find a pursuer who can give an accurate history of back pain.

As is common in such cases, the questions were whether soft tissue injury had accelerated symptoms from an underlying condition and whether there was functional overlay. Based on video surveillance evidence, the court held that there had been deliberate and fraudulent exaggeration and the claim was dismissed. The ultimate award would have been £3,450 before deduction of 25% had the claim been presented truthfully. The sum sought was in excess of £600,000.

An important issue arose in *Sudale v Cyril John Ltd* [2021] 2 WLUK 623 as to the relevance of the defendant's conduct. The claimant had sought damages totalling £232,289. The amount of the award that the court would have made, subject to s.57, was £73,959. In other words, it was on any view a substantial claim. However, the court held that on surveillance evidence demonstrated that the claimant had exaggerated his disability to an extent that amounted to fundamental dishonesty. As a result, the entire claim fell to be dismissed under s.57(2) unless the court was satisfied that the claimant would suffer substantial injustice as a result. In carrying out this exercise, the court refused to consider the potentially dishonest conduct of the defendant on the basis that was an irrelevant factor. In the event that it was a relevant factor, the dishonesty would have had to be at a comparable level to the claimant's to make a difference.

It is not clear that the defender's conduct will be relevant to the question of QOCS protection will be disapplied in Scotland. There is certainly nothing in the regulations or the Act to suggest that the court should look beyond the pursuer's conduct.

There have even been cases where the dishonest claimant has been jailed as a result of section 57. For recent examples see *Calderdale and Huddersfield NHS Trust v Metcalf* [2021] EWHC 611 (QB(6 months imprisonment) and *AXA Insurance UK Plc v Reid* [2021] EWHC 993 (QB) (8 weeks).

CHAPTER SEVEN

IRISH CASELAW

Ireland has a long history of fraudulent and exaggerated personal injury claims, possibly fuelled by the high level of damages awarded in that jurisdiction. That has led to the use of a Personal Injury Assessment Board rather than court procedure for most personal injury claims.

It also led to section 26 of the Civil Liability and Courts Act 2004, which can be seen as the forerunner of section 57 of the 2015 Act. It provides as follows:

> "26.—(1) If, after the commencement of this section, a plaintiff in a personal injuries action gives or adduces, or dishonestly causes to be given or adduced, evidence that—
>
> (*a*) is false or misleading, in any material respect, and
>
> (*b*) he or she knows to be false or misleading,
>
> the court shall dismiss the plaintiff's action unless, for reasons that the court shall state in its decision, the dismissal of the action would result in injustice being done.
>
> (2) The court in a personal injuries action shall, if satisfied that a person has sworn an affidavit under section 14 that
>
> (a) is false or misleading in any material aspect, and
>
> (b) that he or she knew to be false or misleading when swearing the affidavit, dismiss the plaintiff's action unless, for reasons that the court shall state in its decision, the dismissal of the action would result in injustice being done."

In *Ahern v Bus Eireann* [2011] IESC 44 the Supreme Court of Ireland held that understandable exaggeration does not amount to fundamental dishonesty. The onus of proof was on the plaintiff to prove her claim on the balance of probabilities. However, when section 26 of the 2004 Act was raised, the onus of proof lay on the appellant/defendant to prove that false or misleading evidence had been given, also on the balance of probabilities. The High Court judge, who heard all the evidence and could judge the demeanour of the plaintiff, held her to be an honest woman. The Supreme Court was bound to uphold the findings of fact of the trial judge.

In *Farrell v Dublin Bus* [2010] IEHC 327 p75 there was damning surveillance evidence and also evidence that the claimant had worked since the accident, contrary to her claim for loss of earnings. This was her fourth claim for damages for personal injuries and her second against these defenders. It was held that where the claim includes a mixture of genuine and dishonest elements, abandoning the dishonest parts will not necessarily avoid a finding of fundamental dishonesty. The whole action was dismissed.

In *Dunleavy v Swan Park Ltd* 2011 IEHC 232 the court warned that "Section 26 "is there to deter and disallow fraudulent claims. It is not and should not be seen as an opportunity to seize upon anomalies, inconsistencies and unexplained circumstances to avoid a just liability." Such advice is likely to play well with a Scottish court.

CHAPTER EIGHT

TENDERS AND PURSUERS' OFFERS

8.1 Tenders

The law of Scotland has long allowed defenders to protect themselves against the expenses incurred in defending an unreasonable claim by means of lodging a formal offer or tender. The consequences of failing to beat a tender are generally devastating for a pursuer, since it is likely that the expenses of a proof will eat up most if not all of the damages awarded. Even delay in accepting a tender can result in a significant contra-account that comes out of the pursuer's damages.

The fundamental principle is that expressed in *Williamson v McPherson* 1951 SC 438. That case concerned the operation of a tender between defenders as well as between defender and pursuer and the Lord President (Cooper) went back to first principles in determining the outcome (my emphasis added):

> "The point is a novel one which has been thrown into prominence by the provisions of the Law Reform (Miscellaneous Provisions) (Scotland) Act, 1940, which introduces the apportionment of liability as between joint wrongdoers, but it seems to me a question well within the competence of this Court in exercise of the inherent power which we have always asserted to deal by discretionary methods with awards of expenses, and in particular **to do so in such fashion as will ensure that those who cause unnecessary expense are suitably dealt with when the expenses are eventually awarded.**"

This is a principle that will explain most awards of expenses. If a party causes unnecessary expense then they are likely to bear that cost.

8.2 The QOCS Regulations 2021

As noted above, the consequences for a pursuer of failing to beat a tender are usually disastrous. It has long been argued that this puts disproportionate pressure on a pursuer, who is generally less able to absorb the cost of failing to beat a tender than the defender. This has now received statutory recognition in the 2021 Regulations. The pursuer's liability is now restricted to an aggregate sum, payable to all applicants (if more than one) of 75% of the amount of damages awarded to the pursuer, calculated without offsetting against those expenses any expenses due to the pursuer by the applicant, or applicants, before the date of the tender.

Although this mitigates the consequences of failing to beat a tender, and ensures that the pursuer can never be out of pocket, there is still a major incentive to beat the tender. As a result the pursuer and his advisors must still treat any tender with the same degree of caution as they did before.

8.3 Pursuer's Offers

For a long time there was no equivalent provision for a pursuer to put pressure on a defender to settle. An ill-fated attempt to introduce a formal Pursuer's Offer in 1994 was ruled to be ultra vires in *Taylor v Marshalls Food Group Ltd* 1998 SC 841. This was remedied by the Act of Sederunt (Rules of the Court of Session 1994 and Ordinary Cause Rules 1993 Amendment) (Pursuers' Offers) 2017/52 which came into force on 3rd April 2017 and provided as follows:

34A.1. Interpretation of this Chapter

In this Chapter—

"appropriate date" means the date by which a pursuer's offer could reasonably have been accepted;

"fees" means fees of solicitors, and includes any additional fee;

"pursuer's offer" means an offer by a pursuer to settle a claim against a defender made in accordance with this Chapter;

"relevant period" means the period from the appropriate date to the date of acceptance of the pursuer's offer or, as the case may be, to the date on which judgment was given, or on which the verdict was applied.

34A.2.— Pursuers' offers

(1) A pursuer's offer may be made in any cause where the summons includes a conclusion for an order for payment of a sum or sums of money, other than an order—

(a) which the court may not make without evidence; or

(b) the making of which is dependent on the making of another order which the court may not make without evidence.

(2) This Chapter has no effect as regards any other form of offer to settle.

34A.3.— Making of offer

(1) A pursuer's offer is made by lodging in process an offer in the terms specified in rule 34A.4.

(2) A pursuer's offer may be made at any time before—

(a) the court makes avizandum or, if it does not make avizandum, gives judgment; or

(b) in a jury trial, the jury retires to consider the verdict.

(3) A pursuer's offer may be withdrawn at any time before it is accepted by lodging in process a minute of withdrawal.

34A.4.— Form of offer

A pursuer's offer must—

(a) state that it is made under this Chapter;

(b) offer to accept—

(i) a sum or sums of money, inclusive of interest to the date of the offer; and

(ii) the taxed expenses of process; and

(c) specify the conclusion or conclusions of the summons in satisfaction of which the sum or sums and expenses referred to in paragraph (b) would be accepted.

34A.5.— Disclosure of offers

(1) No averment of the fact that a pursuer's offer has been made may be included in any pleadings.

(2) Where a pursuer's offer has not been accepted—

(a) the court must not be informed that an offer has been made until—

(i) the court has pronounced judgment; or

(ii) in the case of a jury trial, the jury has returned its verdict; and

(b) a jury must not be informed that an offer has been made until it has returned its verdict.

34A.6.— Acceptance of offers

(1) A pursuer's offer may be accepted any time before—

(a) the offer is withdrawn;

(b) the court makes avizandum or, if it does not make avizandum, gives judgment; or

(c) in the case of a jury trial, the jury retires to consider its verdict.

(2) It is accepted by lodging in process an acceptance of the offer in the form of a minute of acceptance.

(3) A minute of acceptance must be unqualified other than as respects any question of contribution, indemnity or relief.

(4) On acceptance of a pursuer's offer either the pursuer or the defender may apply by motion for decree in terms of the offer and minute of acceptance.

(5) Where a pursuer's offer includes an offer to accept a sum of money in satisfaction of a conclusion for decree jointly and severally against two or more defenders, the offer is accepted only when accepted by all such defenders.

(6) However, the court may, on the motion of the pursuer, and with the consent of any defender who has lodged a minute of acceptance, grant decree in terms of the offer and minute of acceptance.

34A.7.— Late acceptance of offers

(1) This rule applies to the determination of a motion under rule 34A.6(4) where the court is satisfied that a defender lodged a minute of acceptance after the appropriate date.

(2) On the pursuer's motion the court must, except on cause shown—

(a) allow interest on any sum decerned for from the date on which the pursuer's offer was made; and

(b) find the defender liable for payment to the pursuer of a sum calculated in accordance with rule 34A.9.

(3) Where the court is satisfied that more than one defender lodged a minute of acceptance after the appropriate date the court may find those defenders liable to contribute to payment of the sum referred to in paragraph (2)(b) in such proportions as the court thinks fit.

(4) Where the court makes a finding under paragraph (2)(b), the pursuer may apply for decerniture for payment of the sum as so calculated no later than 21 days after the later of—

(a) the date of the Auditor's report of the taxation of the pursuer's account of expenses; and

(b) the date of the interlocutor disposing of a note of objection.

34A.8.— Non-acceptance of offers

(1) This rule applies where—

(a) a pursuer's offer has been made, and has not been withdrawn;

(b) the offer has not been accepted;

(c) either—

(i) the court has pronounced judgment; or

(ii) in the case of a jury trial, the verdict of the jury has been applied;

(d) the judgment or verdict, in so far as relating to the conclusions of the summons specified in the pursuer's offer, is at least as favourable in money terms to the pursuer as the terms offered; and

(e) the court is satisfied that the pursuer's offer was a genuine attempt to settle the proceedings.

(2) For the purpose of determining if the condition specified in paragraph (1)(d) is satisfied, interest awarded in respect of the period after the lodging of the pursuer's offer is to be disregarded.

(3) On the pursuer's motion the court must, except on cause shown, decern against the defender for payment to the pursuer of a sum calculated in accordance with rule 34A.9.

(4) No such motion may be enrolled after the expiry of 21 days after the later of—

(a) the date of the Auditor's report of the taxation of the pursuer's account of expenses; and

(b) the date of the interlocutor disposing of a note of objection.

(5) Where more than one defender is found liable to the pursuer in respect of a conclusion specified in the offer, the

court may find those defenders liable to contribute to payment of the sum referred to in paragraph (3) in such proportions as it thinks fit.

34A.9. Extent of defender's liability

The sum that may be decerned for under rule 34A.7(2)(b) or rule 34A.8(3) is a sum corresponding to half the fees allowed on taxation of the pursuer's account of expenses, in so far as those fees are attributable to the relevant period, or in so far as they can reasonably be attributed to that period.".

Put shortly, where the pursuer offers to settle for a sum that is less than that ultimately awarded by the court, they are entitled to an uplift of 50% on their expenses incurred since the date of offer (excluding counsels' fees).

In *Anderson v Imrie* 2019 SC 243 the Inner House considered whether a pursuer's offer could take effect in appeal proceedings. Perhaps surprisingly, it was held that a pursuer's offer lodged after determination by the Outer House but before determination of the appeal was incompetent. In that case the pursuer had been successful at first instance and been awarded damages of £325,000. The defenders reclaimed and the pursuer lodged a pursuer's offer of £300,000 (90% of the full value of the award once interest from date of decree was taken into account).

The Inner House refused the pursuer's motion for an uplift on the basis that a Pursuer's Offer could only be lodged before determination of the cause in the Outer House. Given that there is no express provision to this effect, and given that there is no obvious policy objective behind such a reading, the result is difficult to justify. The reasoning is extremely brief: "*[3] In our view the language of Ch 34A is redolent of proceedings in the Outer House. This is consistent with the purpose of encouraging early settlement of personal injury actions. We conclude that Ch 34A pursuers' offers are not available in respect of a challenge to a final decision taken in the Outer House."*

Interestingly, it was accepted that where an interlocutory decision was being reclaimed, a pursuer's offer could still be competent (see para [4]). It is not clear whether this would apply to, for example, dismissal of a claim on the basis of limitation that is successfully reclaimed.

The Inner House also observed that there was force in the defenders' argument that the offer, which was only 10% less than the sum awarded at first instance, was not a "genuine offer to settle" in terms of 34A.8.1(e).

This does not mean that a pursuer's offer has no effect during appellate proceedings. So long as the offer was lodged before the determination at first instance, then there is no reason why the "relevant period" during which expenses are calculated should exclude appellate procedure. An illustration of this can be found in the case of *Wright v National Galleries of Scotland* (No. 2) 2020 Rep LR 126. In that case the defenders were assoilzied at first instance but the pursuer was successful on appeal to the Sheriff Appeal Court. The pursuer had lodged a pursuer's offer in terms of Chapter 27 of the Ordinary Cause Rules 1993 that was slightly lower than the ultimate award. The defenders argued that relevant period did not include appeal proceedings on the basis of the *Imrie* decision. The Sheriff Appeal Court held that *"the obvious purpose of the pursuer's offer is to provide another mechanism to facilitate settlement and in particular early settlement of the action. That purpose would be undermined if a pursuer who had lodged an offer to settle prior to proof cannot avail himself of the rule which requires the court to decern against the defender for payment of a specific sum or liability as specified in OCR 27A.9 provided the judgment is at least as favourable in money terms to the pursuer as the terms offered. in our opinion it does not matter whether the judgment which is at least as favourable in money terms to the pursuer is the sheriff's judgment following proof or the judgment of this court following an appeal against the sheriff's decision on liability and/or quantum. The purpose and provisions of Chapter 27A can be put into effect by this court on appeal."*

8.4 Extra judicial offers

Even where an offer is not formal, it may still have an impact on expenses and so cannot be safely ignored. If nothing else, it may be grounds for an additional fee (see above and *Cameron v Kvaerner Govan Ltd* 1999 SLT 638, where the pursuer was granted an additional fee under head (g) on account of having made an offer to settle that should have been accepted).

The defenders may also rely on an extra-judicial offer, even though the consequences are less clear cut than if a tender had been lodged. In *Spence v Wilson (No 2)* 1998 SLT 959 the pursuer received damages of £10,805 in 1998, having rejected a tender for £40,000 in 1995. However, the law in relation to recoverable benefits had altered in the interim, due to section 15 of the Social Security (Recovery of Benefits) Act 1997. As a result, it was held that the tender was no longer competent as it did not specify how much the pursuer would receive after deduction of recoupable benefits. The Lord Ordinary held that this rendered the tender ineffective. However, he could still take account of the fact that the pursuer should have accepted the offer in 1995 in assessing expenses, and made no award of expenses due to or by either party.

CHAPTER NINE

RECOVERY OF JUDICIAL EXPENSES

9.1 <u>The general rule</u>

The starting point is that "expenses follow success". In J A Maclaren (1912), *Expenses in the Supreme and Sheriff Courts*, p 21, the principle is laid down upon the authority of a number of cases that *"if any party is put to expense in vindicating his rights, he is entitled to recover it from the person by whom it was created, unless there is something in his own conduct that gives him the character of an improper litigant in insisting on things which his title does not warrant."*

However, in practice the successful party seldom recovers in full the cost of litigation. The extent to which the successful party remains out of pocket depends on the mode of taxation of expenses.

9.2 <u>Modes of taxation: party and party; solicitor and client, client paying; or solicitor and client, third party paying</u>

By far the most common form of taxation is party and party. In such a taxation only such expenses are allowed as are reasonable for conducting the litigation in a proper manner. Where a taxation is to be as between party and party a solicitor has the option, unless the table of fees otherwise provides, of charging his account on the basis either of the inclusive fees or of the detailed fees in the table, but he cannot make charges partly on the one basis and partly on the other. Where counsel is employed, counsel's fees and fees for the instruction of counsel are allowed only where the court has sanctioned the employment of counsel. In practice, a significant proportion of expenses incurred are not recoverable on this basis.

Expenses on an agent and client basis are far more generous although seldom awarded. The test for awarded expenses on an agent/client basis was set out by Lord Hodge, then in the Outer House, in the case of *McKie v The Scottish Minsters* 2006 SC 528:

> "The law on this issue is well settled and may be summarised in the following five propositions. First, the court has discretion as to the scale of expenses which should be awarded. Secondly, in the normal case expenses are awarded on a party and party scale; that scale applies in the absence of any specification to the contrary. But, thirdly, where one of the parties has conducted the litigation incompetently or unreasonably, and thereby caused the other party unnecessary expense, the court can impose, as a sanction against such conduct, an award of expenses on the solicitor and client scale. Fourthly, in its consideration of the reasonableness of a party's conduct of an action, the court can take into account all relevant circumstances. Those circumstances include the party's behaviour before the action commenced, the adequacy of a party's preparation for the action, the strengths or otherwise of a party's position on the substantive merits of the action, the use of a court action for an improper purpose, and the way in which a party has used court procedure, for example to progress or delay the resolution of the dispute. Fifthly, where the court has awarded expenses at an earlier stage in the proceedings without reserving for later determination the scale of such expenses, any award of expenses on the solicitor and client scale may cover only those matters not already covered by the earlier awards."

9.3 Additional fee/charge

Partly in recognition of the fact that a solicitor will seldom recover the full costs of running an action, however successfully, there is provision in both the Court of Session and the sheriff court for an uplift. Traditionally this was a highly opaque procedure and it was almost impossible to predict (1) whether an additional fee would be allowed at all and (2) if so, how that would translate into a monetary sum. In an attempt to make the process more transparent, the Court of Session rules have been amended to bring them into line with sheriff court practice, where a percentage uplift is awarded. The uplift is now called an additional charge rather than an additional fee. For actions raised after 29th April 2019 the Act of Sederunt (Taxation of Judicial Expenses Rules) 2019 provides as follows:

5.2.— Additional charge

(1) An entitled party may apply to the court for an increase in the charges to be allowed at taxation in respect of work carried out by the entitled party's solicitor.

(2) Where the application is made to the Court of Session the court may, instead of determining the application, remit the application to the Auditor to determine if an increase should be allowed, and the level of any increase.

(3) The court or, as the case may be, the Auditor must grant the application when satisfied that an increase is justified to reflect the responsibility undertaken by the solicitor in the conduct of the proceedings.

(4) On granting an application the court must, subject to paragraph (5), specify a percentage increase in the charges to be allowed at taxation.

(5) The Court of Session may instead remit to the Auditor to determine the level of increase.

(6) In considering whether to grant an application, and the level of any increase, the court or, as the case may be, the Auditor is to have regard to—

(a) the complexity of the proceedings and the number, difficulty or novelty of the questions raised;

(b) the skill, time and labour and specialised knowledge required of the solicitor;

(c) the number and importance of any documents prepared or perused;

(d) the place and circumstances of the proceedings or in which the work of the solicitor in preparation for, and conduct of, the proceedings has been carried out;

(e) the importance of the proceedings or the subject matter of the proceedings to the client;

(f) the amount or value of money or property involved in the proceedings;

(g) the steps taken with a view to settling the proceedings, limiting the matters in dispute or limiting the scope of any hearing.

In the first case to consider these new provisions, *Rev Philip and ors v Scottish Minsters* [2021] CSOH 52 Lord Braid held that having heard the petition the court was better placed than the auditor to determine both whether an uplift should be granted and, if so, the extent of it. The petitioners sought an uplift of 100% and the respondents, whilst accepting that a modest uplift was appropriate, argued that the extent of that should be determined by the auditor. Lord Braid awarded an uplift of 50%.

It is hoped that the new rules will provide a body of case law by which practitioners are better placed to predict future awards.

9.4 Exceptions to the general rule

There are two broad categories of exception to the general rule that expenses follow success. The first arises where there has been mixed or divided expense. The second is where the court wishes to mark its disapproval of some aspect of a litigant's conduct.

Both issues arose in *Ramm v Lothian and Borders Fire Board* SC 226. The pursuer sued his employers for injuries sustained at work and quantum was agreed at £2,065. Liability was established subject to contributory negligence of two thirds. No tender or offer had been made by the defenders. The pursuer failed on the ground of action that had taken up most time at proof and which had greatest wider implications. The Lord Ordinary made an award of no expenses due to or by either party, principally on the basis that *"The evidence in this case demonstrated that the pursuer had initiated and insisted in a case against the defenders themselves for which there was, at best, inadequate evidence and never any evidence of substance."*

The Inner House refused the reclaiming motion. Although the Lord Ordinary should have explicitly recognised that the starting point should be that expenses normally follow success, this was not fatal to his decision and he was best placed to decide how much time had been wasted on the matters on which the pursuer had failed.

An even more extreme (and unusual) decision illustrating these exceptions is *Grubb v Finlay* 2017 [CSOH] 81. This was a particularly acrimonious litigation in the Court of Session that lasted many days over several diets of proof.

The claim related to a low velocity impact on a garage forecourt which the pursuer claimed had caused him significant functional disability. There was a substantial body of evidence demonstrating that the pursuer was exaggerating his disability. A tender was lodged and withdrawn. The final award was for solatium only based on 12 months of symptoms. The damages awarded were £7,321.31, including interest, as opposed to the £182,880.80 sought.

The defenders sought dismissal of the action at common law (section 57 does not apply in Scotland). That motion was refused. On the basis of the cases referred to above, it seems very likely that the motion would have succeeded in England.

However, when the pursuer moved for the expenses of the action, the expenses were actually awarded to the defenders, subject to a discount of one third. As far as I am aware, this is the only example of an award of expenses in a personal injuries litigation in favour of the unsuccessful party.

When the case came to the Inner House (2018 SLT 463) both reclaiming motions were refused, largely on the basis that these were issues primarily for the judge at first instance with which an appellate court should be slow to interfere. There was clearly some hesitancy about the finding on expenses:

> "38 The Lord Ordinary's award in favour of the defenders is, at first sight, a surprising one. After all, the defenders had declined to lodge a tender (after withdrawal of an earlier one). In normal circumstances, the rules applicable to tenders ought to be applied, even where the award is small (if not de minimis). The rules on tenders ought not to be lightly departed from (see Lord Carloway in Macfadyen ed: Court of Session Practice (L/105) para [104]). Expenses ought normally to follow success, and the pursuer was successful in that he achieved an award in his favour."

However, it was accepted that there was material before the Lord Ordinary to justify this unusual result and that had the pursuer been candid any proof (if required at all) would have been far shorter and less expensive.

The danger of decisions such as these – and the reason that they are so rare – is that they sacrifice uniformity and predictability. They are also likely to promote satellite litigation and, as noted below, are difficult to cure on appeal.

CHAPTER TEN

QOCS APPEALS

10.1 The conventional approach

Traditionally Scottish courts have been extremely reluctant to entertain appeals in relation to expenses. Expenses are seen as very much a matter of discretion for the judge at first instance. As the Inner House explained in *Grubb v Finlay* (see above):

> "*37. Appeals on expenses "should not be entertained except where there has been an obvious miscarriage of justice" (Lord Advocate v Mackie 2016 SLT 118, LJC (Carloway) at para [11], following Miller v Chivas Bros 2015 SC 85, Lady Dorrian, delivering the Opinion of the Court, at para [23], citing Caldwell v Dykes (1906) 8 F 839, LP (Dunedin) at 840). Awards of expenses are discretionary and will only be reversed upon the conventional grounds applicable to the exercise of a discretion. The appellate court must take care not to substitute its own view, based on the limited, printed material in the process before it, in contrast to the first instance judge's complete knowledge and understanding of the whole proceedings before him or her.*"

In similar vein, Macphail's Sheriff Court Practice notes at 18.117 that "*In practice, however, appeals solely on questions of expenses are severely discouraged, and are not entertained unless either there has been an obvious miscarriage of justice, or the expenses have become a great deal more valuable than the merits, or a question of principle is involved.*"

It might be thought that the courts would be particularly reluctant to interfere with findings in relation to QOCS, which involve not just questions of expenses but also assessment of credibility and reliability. Such matters are only amenable to appeal where the judge at first instance is "plainly wrong" – see *Thomson v Kvaerner Govan Ltd* 2004 SC(HL) 1; *Henderson v Foxworth Investments* 2014 SC UKSC 203; *McGraddie v McGraddie* 2014 SC (UKSC) 12.

10.2 Appeals under the new regime

It may well be that where practice is developing, as it will be in relation to issues like QOCS, the appeal courts will be less reticent about intervening in order to lay down general principles. That certainly seems to be the case in England and Wales, where appellate courts have not been so slow to interfere.

For example, in *Molodi* (see above) the court appears to have been attracted to the distinction between a finding of pure fact, such as credibility, and the inference to be drawn from ascertained primary facts, such as whether the pursuer had been fundamentally dishonest

There is some echo of this in the opinion of Lord Drummond Young in *Anderson v Imrie* 2018 SC where he suggested that the degree to which an appellate court could interfere with a decision at first instance would depend on how much the trial judge had benefitted from seeing and hearing the evidence at first hand.

It should be noted that Lord Brodie, whilst accepting a distinction between a pure question of fact and a mixed question of fact and law, felt that the "plainly wrong" test applied to both.

CHAPTER ELEVEN

CONCLUSIONS AND POSSIBLE FUTURE DEVELOPMENTS

There have been extensive changes in practice and procedure relating to the funding of personal injury litigation in Scotland in the last 20 years. Those changes are going to accelerate in the next few years and to a large extent we are now in unchartered territory. Although we have English and Welsh caselaw to assist, those cases have to be treated with caution given the considerable differences in wording of the relevant rules and legislation and the different litigation culture.

The biggest unknown is whether greater access to litigation will lead to more fraudulent or exaggerated claims. There is no doubt that constant publicising of compensation claims has made the public less anxious about consulting a lawyer in the first place. The widespread use of remote hearings during the Covid pandemic has already lead to greater informality in court procedure. There are benefits to this but also dangers.

Going forward, will we see an equivalent to section 57 of the 2015 Act in Scotland? Will the courts become more willing to exercise their common law power to dismiss a claim on the grounds of fundamental dishonesty (see *Summers v Fairclough Homes* [2012] 1 WLR 2004)? At present, the courts have shown little interest in such an approach, as demonstrated by *Grubb v Finlay* where an attempt to have the action dismissed for fundamental dishonesty was refused. That lack of interest may well now change.

MORE BOOKS BY
LAW BRIEF PUBLISHING

A selection of our other titles available now:-

'A Practical Guide to Solicitor and Client Costs – 2nd Edition' by Robin Dunne
'Constructive Dismissal – Practice Pointers and Principles' by Benjimin Burgher
'A Practical Guide to Religion and Belief Discrimination Claims in the Workplace' by Kashif Ali
'A Practical Guide to the Law of Medical Treatment Decisions' by Ben Troke
'Fundamental Dishonesty and QOCS in Personal Injury Proceedings: Law and Practice' by Jake Rowley
'A Practical Guide to the Law in Relation to School Exclusions' by Charlotte Hadfield & Alice de Coverley
'A Practical Guide to Divorce for the Silver Separators' by Karin Walker
'The Right to be Forgotten – The Law and Practical Issues' by Melissa Stock
'A Practical Guide to Planning Law and Rights of Way in National Parks, the Broads and AONBs' by James Maurici QC, James Neill et al
'A Practical Guide to Election Law' by Tom Tabori
'A Practical Guide to the Law in Relation to Surrogacy' by Andrew Powell
'A Practical Guide to Claims Arising from Fatal Accidents – 2nd Edition' by James Patience
'A Practical Guide to the Ownership of Employee Inventions – From Entitlement to Compensation' by James Tumbridge & Ashley Roughton
'A Practical Guide to Asbestos Claims' by Jonathan Owen & Gareth McAloon
'A Practical Guide to Stamp Duty Land Tax in England and Northern Ireland' by Suzanne O'Hara
'A Practical Guide to the Law of Farming Partnerships' by Philip Whitcomb

'Covid-19, Homeworking and the Law – The Essential Guide to Employment and GDPR Issues' by Forbes Solicitors

'Covid-19, Force Majeure and Frustration of Contracts – The Essential Guide' by Keith Markham

'Covid-19 and Criminal Law – The Essential Guide' by Ramya Nagesh

'Covid-19 and Family Law in England and Wales – The Essential Guide' by Safda Mahmood

'A Practical Guide to the Law of Unlawful Eviction and Harassment – 2nd Edition' by Stephanie Lovegrove

'Covid-19, Residential Property, Equity Release and Enfranchisement – The Essential Guide' by Paul Sams and Louise Uphill

'Covid-19, Brexit and the Law of Commercial Leases – The Essential Guide' by Mark Shelton

'A Practical Guide to Costs in Personal Injury Claims – 2nd Edition' by Matthew Hoe

'A Practical Guide to the General Data Protection Regulation (GDPR) – 2nd Edition' by Keith Markham

'Ellis on Credit Hire – Sixth Edition' by Aidan Ellis & Tim Kevan

'A Practical Guide to Working with Litigants in Person and McKenzie Friends in Family Cases' by Stuart Barlow

'Protecting Unregistered Brands: A Practical Guide to the Law of Passing Off' by Lorna Brazell

'A Practical Guide to Secondary Liability and Joint Enterprise Post-Jogee' by Joanne Cecil & James Mehigan

'A Practical Guide to the Pre-Action RTA Claims Protocol for Personal Injury Lawyers' by Antonia Ford

'A Practical Guide to Neighbour Disputes and the Law' by Alexander Walsh

'A Practical Guide to Forfeiture of Leases' by Mark Shelton

'A Practical Guide to Coercive Control for Legal Practitioners and Victims' by Rachel Horman

'A Practical Guide to Financial Ombudsman Service Claims'
by Adam Temple & Robert Scrivenor

'A Practical Guide to Advising Schools on Employment Law' by Jonathan Holden

'A Practical Guide to Running Housing Disrepair and Cavity Wall Claims:
2nd Edition' by Andrew Mckie & Ian Skeate

'A Practical Guide to Holiday Sickness Claims – 2nd Edition'
by Andrew Mckie & Ian Skeate

'Arguments and Tactics for Personal Injury and Clinical Negligence Claims'
by Dorian Williams

'A Practical Guide to Drone Law' by Rufus Ballaster, Andrew Firman, Eleanor Clot

'A Practical Guide to Compliance for Personal Injury Firms Working With Claims
Management Companies' by Paul Bennett

'A Practical Guide to Dog Law for Owners and Others' by Andrea Pitt

'RTA Allegations of Fraud in a Post-Jackson Era: The Handbook – 2nd Edition'
by Andrew Mckie

'RTA Personal Injury Claims: A Practical Guide Post-Jackson' by Andrew Mckie

'On Experts: CPR35 for Lawyers and Experts' by David Boyle

'An Introduction to Personal Injury Law' by David Boyle

'A Practical Guide to Subtle Brain Injury Claims' by Pankaj Madan

These books and more are available to order online direct from the publisher at www.lawbriefpublishing.com, where you can also read free sample chapters. For any queries, contact us on 0844 587 2383 or mail@lawbriefpublishing.com.

Our books are also usually in stock at www.amazon.co.uk with free next day delivery for Prime members, and at good legal bookshops such as Wildy & Sons.

We are regularly launching new books in our series of practical day-to-day practitioners' guides. Visit our website and join our free newsletter to be kept informed and to receive special offers, free chapters, etc.

You can also follow us on Twitter at www.twitter.com/lawbriefpub.